A PORTFOLIO OF

CERAMIC &NATURAL TILE IDEAS

CONTENTS

What Makes a Great Tile Idea ? 5

Planning 7

Where to Use Tile 7

Choosing the Right Tile 10

Floor Tiles 12

Wall Tiles 18

Counter Tiles 26

Design 33

Designing with Tile 33

Shape & Size 34

Color 36

Pattern & Texture 38

Art Tiles 40

Decorated Tiles 42

Natural Tiles 46

Mosaic Tiles 50

Relief Tiles 52

A Portfolio of Ceramic & Natural Tile Ideas 55

Tile in the Bathroom 57

Tile in the Kitchen 65

Tile in Common Living Areas 73

Tile Outdoors 89

List of Contributors 96

© Copyright 1996
Cy DeCosse Incorporated
5900 Green Oak Drive
Minnetonka, Minnesota 55343
1-800-328-3895
All rights reserved

Library of Congress
Cataloging-in-Publication Data
Portfolio of ceramic & natural tile ideas.
p. cm.

ISBN 0-86573-991-9 (softcover)
1. Tiles in interior decoration.
I. Cy DeCosse Incorporated.
NK2115.5.T54P67 1996
747'.9—dc20
96-15845   CIP

Author: Home How-To Institute™
Creative Director: William B. Jones
Associate Creative Director: Tim Himsel
Group Executive Editor: Paul Currie
Managing Editor: Carol Harvatin
Assistant Project Manager: Andrew Sweet
Art Director: Ruth Eischens
Copy Editor: Janice Cauley
Vice President of Photography & Production: Jim Bindas
Production Coordinator: Laura Hokkanen
Printed on American paper by Webcrafters Inc. (0796)
CY DECOSSE INCORPORATED

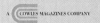
A COWLES MAGAZINES COMPANY

Chairman/CEO: Bruce Barnet
Chairman Emeritus: Cy DeCosse
President/COO: Nino Tarantino
Executive V.P./Editor-in-Chief: William B. Jones
99 98 97 96 / 5 4 3 2 1

Photos on page two (top to bottom) courtesy of Florida Tile
Industries Inc., Ann Sacks Tile & Stone, American Olean.
Photos on page three (top to bottom) courtesy of United States
Ceramic Tile Co., Florida Tile Industries Inc., Crossville Ceramics.

A well-chosen mixture of the various types of tile is beautifully blended together in this classically elegant bathroom. The same marbleized beige finish is carried on the floor tiles, the wall tiles, the countertop and the trim tiles around the sink to create a unified look. Behind the sink, a decorative border of stylized green ceramic tiles and modeled relief trim create a backsplash that is wonderfully striking and water-resistant as well.

WHAT MAKES A GREAT TILE IDEA?

Ceramic tile offers almost limitless possibilities as a surface covering. It allows you to be inventive and creative, yet remains very functional in almost all applications. *A Portfolio of Ceramic & Natural Tile Ideas* will show you some of the most effective ways to use ceramic tile and help you plan your own great tile installation. It will show you how beautifully ceramic tile can work into your rooms and give you photos to refer to when making important decorating decisions with tile.

Ceramic and natural tile have an impressive history. Tile has been used as an element of decoration and architecture for more than 12,000 years. Archeological digs along the Nile have uncovered ceramic tiles, thousands of years old, that were as beautiful as if they had been recently installed. Advancements in ceramic and natural tile production have made tile more affordable and easier to install—today it is more popular than ever before.

Aesthetically, there are few surfacing materials that can have the dramatic impact of ceramic tile. The range of colors, sizes, shapes and textures makes ceramic tiles an easy way to create a unique effect and brighten any room. The beauty and durability of ceramic or natural tile will also add to the value of your home.

You find the perfect combination of beauty, practicality and function when you choose tile to finish any area. Ceramic tiles provide a surface that is fireproof, durable, soil and moisture-resistant and easy to keep.

Ceramic tile can be fun as well as functional. Here, a complex design, just below the edge of a counter, was composed of ceramic art tiles, which have a distinctive relief design. Framed by small matching blue ceramic tiles, the primitive animal images can be used as a decorative accent, or as part of a design theme that is carried throughout the room.

The rich beauty of polished marble creates a tile floor surface that is handsome and hard-wearing. In this eloquent example, geometric patterns and subtle earth-tone colors create an incredible tile design that visually guides you from one area to another.

Planning
WHERE TO USE TILE

Tiles are a functional and efficient choice for almost any surface application, especially floors, walls and countertops. Ceramic and natural tiles are effective choices for a number of areas around the home. They are ideal for wet areas, such as bathrooms and kitchens, and areas that take the abuse of heavy traffic and lots of use, such as floors and walls and kitchen countertops. Tiles are tough, easy to clean, water-resistant and fireproof, and are available in an amazing selection of colors, shapes, sizes, textures and patterns.

Ceramic tile has limitless possibilities in both design and application. A tiled floor, wall or counter can last as long as your house if the original installation is done properly. If you need to replace damaged tiles, or simply want to change the design for aesthetic reasons, individual tiles can be replaced, or added onto, without having to remove the entire installation.

Although tile is used most often in bathrooms and kitchens, it has a number of other practical applications as well. Tile can be installed on vertical or horizontal surfaces, indoors or outside, and can withstand extreme temperatures and exposure to water. It makes a practical and attractive floor for a high-traffic entry area or family room. Tile can also be used as a colorful accent, an easy-to-clean surface on a countertop or table, or a great-looking, heat-resistant surface surrounding a fireplace.

Tile is also an efficient solar energy collector. When installed as flooring for a sunroom or greenhouse, natural and ceramic tile will retain and radiate heat, making it one of the most versatile floor coverings you can install. Natural tiles are better heat conductors than ceramic, but both materials have some heat-storing properties. In the winter, tile stores heat from sunlight during the day and slowly releases it at night. In the summer, tile helps cool an area. If kept shaded and away from sunlight, a tile floor and surrounding space will stay cooler.

Because of its good looks and formal appeal, many people think of ceramic tile as a luxury. The major cost factor with ceramic tile is the cost of installation. The materials are actually very affordable. The cost of materials for a ceramic floor can be about the same as a vinyl floor, but tile will outlast vinyl, making it a more cost-efficient material in the long run. Many tiles are also water-resistant, so they are suitable for a wider range of applications. You can offset some of the installation cost by installing the tile yourself, but because ceramic tile can be tricky to work with, many people turn to professionals for help and advice.

A wide selection of trim and border tiles is available to match almost any line of tile products. Border tiles are used to finish out the edges and corners of countertops, backsplashes and walls and to form a smooth transition where floors and walls meet. Trim tiles add colorful and decorative accents to a tile design. When choosing trim tiles, bring along samples of the other tiles, colors and materials you will to be using them with.

WHERE TO USE TILE

There are certain areas in your home where it makes good sense to use ceramic or natural tile on a surface, depending on its function and use in the space. For example, a countertop bar in a den functions primarily as a place to set drinks and would benefit from a ceramic tile surface, as would a heavily used countertop located next to a busy kitchen sink.

Tile can enhance a space a number of different ways. Decorative tile in an entry gives your home a welcome appeal. Tile in the kitchen provides a decorative and durable surface on countertops, backsplashes and kick plates, as well as on floors and walls. In a bathroom, ceramic tile can brighten the space and give it a fresh new look. It can be used on the tub or shower surround, walls, floors and countertops, not to mention as an attractive accent and design element. Because tile can withstand intense heat and is easy to clean, ceramic tile is also an excellent choice for fireplace mantels, hearths and facings.

The determining factor in choosing the correct tile is how much moisture resistance the tiled area will require. "Wet areas" are surfaces that are subjected to a great deal of moisture or liquid. Indoor wet areas include: countertops that contain sinks, tub enclosures, showers, laundry rooms, saunas and swimming pools. Ceramic tiles installed in these wet areas must be water-resistant, and the setting materials must be able to tolerate moisture. The subsurface must be water-resistant as well.

All exterior locations are considered wet areas. Tiles installed outdoors must be able to withstand significant changes in temperature without cracking or heaving. Colder climates require that exterior tiles have the stability to resist constant freezing and thawing.

Tile glaze, texture and thickness are dependent on where you decide to install ceramic tile—floor applications and heavily used countertops require a glazed tile, which is harder and more resistant to wear. Ceramic tiles used on floors have a nonslip surface, whether they are glazed or unglazed. Walls and countertops that don't get used as heavily don't require a tile with as much durability.

Tiles used in outdoor applications, such as around pool areas, patios and porch floors, should have a nonslip surface and the ability to endure extreme temperature changes. Quarry pavers are an excellent choice for use in these areas. They are attractive and durable. Avoid using polished stone or large smooth tiles for any floor near water, whether it is indoors or outside—these materials can be dangerously slippery when wet.

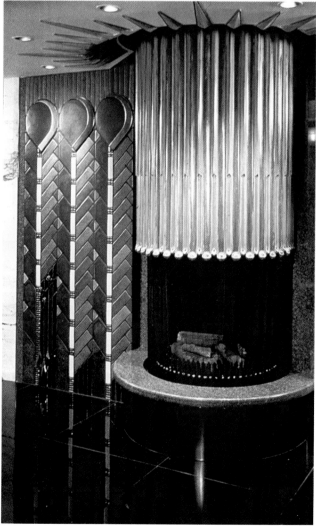

Photo courtesy of David Ellison, St. Clair Shores, MI. Photo by Gary Quesada, Balthazar Korab Ltd., Tile Heritage Foundation

Festive and fire-resistant, *the ceramic tile used around this fireplace brings you the best of both worlds. The vividly colorful ceramic tile design makes a striking visual statement. In contrast, the hearth, mantel and floor in front of the fireplace opening have the subtle colors and textures of natural marble and granite.*

Floor tile, with the earthy appeal of naturally weathered stone, complements the neutral colors of the cabinetry. A collection of decorative tiles, with a clever country-style motif, creates a washable, water-resistant surface for the backsplash.

The crisp, clean look of white ceramic brightens any setting. In a small bathroom, the simple beauty of the gleaming white tile can be used to enlarge the sense of space. These plain white tiles were embellished with a border of soft pastel-colored floral print tiles, and edged with decorative braid trim.

Tiles made from natural stone provide deep, rich colors and a very protective surface for this floor. The rough texture of the natural stone makes these floor tiles a safe choice because they're more slip-resistant than a smooth, glossy tile.

In this lavish lavatory, you'll find a type of tile for every possible function. Textured tile on the floor creates a slip-resistant surface, ceramic wall tiles provide water-resistant protection around the tub, and decorative trim and accent tiles form mosaic-style borders that add a dramatic flair and visually tie the setting together.

CHOOSING THE RIGHT TILE

Because the selection of tile types is so diverse, you can find ceramic and natural tile that is appropriate for almost any application imaginable. The key is selecting the right tile for the right job. Whether you're choosing tile for a shower area, a countertop or an entryway, there will be plenty of options for the type of ceramic tile that fits your lifestyle needs.

Ceramic and natural tiles can be used in new construction or renovations. They make durable and decorative surfaces for floors, walls, countertops, tables, fireplaces, stairways and ceilings. You can use tile to cover surfaces that are straight or curved, cornered or angular. There's hardly an interior setting where ceramic or natural tile couldn't be used. Outside the house, ceramic and natural tile are excellent choices for patios, pool surrounds and hot tub areas, fountains and water gardens.

Because of its formal appeal and historic ties to royalty and places of worship, many people consider ceramic tile a luxury, when in reality it is a very affordable option. For example, the cost of material for a ceramic floor is about the same as a vinyl floor. The installation cost will be more expensive for ceramic tile, but it will last much longer, spreading the cost out over a longer period of time and in the long run be more cost effective. Tiling a wall or countertop will be more costly initially than painting, hanging wallpaper or installing plastic laminate, but the tile will still look good when the other materials are faded and worn and ready to be replaced. And because ceramic and natural tiles are more resistant to water than other materials, they are more practical for almost all residential applications.

Grout is used to support and protect the edges of the tile, not to affix it to the subsurface. Although it is not considered part of the design process, selecting the proper grout can make a dramatic difference in the look and performance of a ceramic tile application. There is a wide selection of grout colors to choose from. There basically two types of grout; cement-based and epoxy grouts. Cement based grouts are cheaper and are water-resistant, but not absolutely waterproof. Epoxy

grouts are highly waterproof and resistant to most stains. Each type has varying performance characteristics; the type you choose will depend on the design scheme and level of use.

Ceramic and natural stone walls, floors and countertops are easy to care for, especially when stain-resistant grout is used. Tile floors should be swept or vacuumed on a regular basis to remove gritty particles that may cause scratching. Ceramic floors can be cleaned by wiping them with a damp mop or sponge. Even when they are neglected for a long time, the lustrous sheen can usually be brought back with a good washing.

Tile is also easy to replace if needed. When wall-to-wall carpeting gets a burn, you usually have to replace the entire piece. However, if damage occurs to a tiled floor, cracked or loose tiles and damaged grout can easily be repaired without tearing out the entire installation. If you want to make changes for aesthetic reasons, most tile installations can be restyled, accented or added to without removing all of the existing tile.

The warm tones and rough texture of these Italian ceramic tiles gives them an old-world appearance. A mosaic-style design uses pieces of the same earth-tone tiles, giving the setting a rich, refined appearance.

Ceramic tile has more practical applications and natural elegance *than almost any surface material imaginable. An array of ceramic tiles is combined to create a relaxed, contemporary interior that has a casual elegance and is also practical and easy to care for. Stylish ceramic tiles protect the countertop and add a polished sophistication to the area surrounding this wet bar.*

New sealants and waxes can add labor-saving finishes to tiles used in areas that get especially hard wear, such as entryways and hallways.

Choosing the right tile

FLOOR TILES

Ceramic and natural tiles are strong, colorfast, water-resistant and easy to clean. They are a natural choice for floor surfaces. Ceramic floor tiles are thicker and more durable than wall tiles because they need to be able to handle heavy traffic in wet entryways, and drips and spills in kitchens and bathrooms.

The first thing to consider when choosing a floor tile is how much exposure to moisture the surface will get. Next, determine the amount of foot traffic and wear the surface will have to endure. Ceramic floor tiles should have either a glazed, or partially glazed surface. Unglazed tiles are not as water-resistant or as dense. Glazed tiles have a ceramic coating fired onto them at high temperatures, which makes them stronger.

When selecting glazed floor tiles it is important to choose a tile with a glaze that is appropriate for the location and level of wear it will need to withstand. Glazed floor tiles are rated by the manufacturer according to resistance to wear in various applications. Look for tiles whose wear rating matches the needs of the floor you are going to tile. Although tile is very hard and durable, some areas, such as kitchen countertops, where chopping of hard objects occurs, have a higher risk of breakage.

Tile is classified as light traffic, medium traffic, heavy traffic and commercial. "Light traffic" tile is for areas that are walked on with soft footwear or bare feet. Because they don't need to tolerate as much wear, light traffic tiles don't need to be as strong or as durable as tiles in other applications. "Medium traffic" tile is able to handle normal footwear and has a medium resistance to scratching. This is not a tile for heavy traffic areas, where dirt and grit are dragged in from outside. "Heavy traffic" tile is acceptable for most residential and light commercial applications. This is the rating you should look for when choosing tile for entryways, kitchens, balconies and terraces, as well as a number of other areas, both indoors and out. "Commercial" tiles are also suitable for many residential applications.

The uniform shape and small size of these floor tiles creates a pattern that pulls the space together. The simplicity of the pattern keeps the look clean and simple.

The rough and rustic look of the massive stone walls and ceiling is beautifully balanced by smooth stone floor tiles. A marbled white border adds an elegant accent and frames this unusual, but very captivating, combination.

Hard-wearing ceramic floor tiles are a long-lasting option for busy places like playrooms. And if anyone gets a bit creative with a crayon, ceramic tiles are also easy to clean.

A colorful and creative use of ceramic tile creates a fashionable and functional floor. A dynamic pattern combines rich colors and textures to create the look of an elegant area rug and denotes the central activity area of this kitchen.

FLOOR TILES

Another important factor to consider when choosing floor tiles is the level of slip resistance that is needed. Two things affect the degree of slip resistance required: the amount of water and environmental factors. The greater chance your floor has of being exposed to water or household spills, the greater the need for slip-resistant tiles. Your need for slip-resistant tiles will also be determined by your family's lifestyle needs. For example, floors that will be used by small children, people who are physically challenged or the elderly require floor tiles with definite slip-resistant characteristics.

Floor tiles in an entryway require a surface that won't be slippery when wet, whether they are glazed or unglazed. Use glazed floor tiles with a matte finish for the areas around a shower or tub, and make sure the tile is textured for slip resistance. A tile with a glossy finish has more tendency to be slippery when wet.

Steps and stairways are other surfaces where a ceramic tile application can become one of the most dramatic elements in your home. For applications on steps and stairs it is important to take safety into account. For the treads of a stairway, select sturdy floor tiles with a textured surface. Use trim pieces to define the edges of the steps, or trim the edges with wood. With accented risers, each step is clearly defined and much safer. Install tiles across the full width of the riser, or set individual tiles as a riser accent.

Ceramic tile floors are long-lasting and easy to clean. They can also be hard and cold underfoot. Strategically placed rugs, in front of sinks and work counters, soften the look of the hard surface and minimize the impact of the cold tile.

(inset photo above) **Uniquely shaped floor and mosaic tiles** *are combined in a colorful and creative design that becomes the centerpiece of this room.*

(left) **The rich colors and precise patterns** *that comprise this polished ceramic floor design add warmth and animation to its elegant appeal.*

FLOOR TILES

Climate conditions must be considered when choosing a floor tile that will have an outdoor application. Installing tile outdoors requires a tile that is frost-resistant. If you live in a climate where the ground freezes, select a type of tile that can withstand extreme changes in temperature.

Tiles for outdoor use should be textured and slip-resistant. Glazed ceramic, cut stone, terra-cotta and mosaic tiles are some of the high-quality, long-wearing tiles that bring the natural beauty of tile to an outdoor setting.

When installing patio tiles, remember to slope the site so the paved areas will drain quickly and puddles won't form.

Photo courtesy of Crossville Ceramics

The colorful mosaic tile design *in this floor adds a dynamic accent to the small space. The combination of colors and shapes gives the mosaic design the illusion of being three-dimensional.*

Photo courtesy of Crossville Ceramics

Not just a protective floor surface, *polished ceramic creates an entryway that is pure elegance. The gleaming, high-gloss tile used in the entryway extends this protective surface into the kitchen as well.*

Photo courtesy of Sicis, Rex, Gabbianelli, Bardelli, Mayo De Lucci, Italian Trade Commission - Tile Center in New York

The uneven coloring *of the marble floor tiles creates a textured effect within the bands of color. Crisp white ceramic tile is used to create a contrast and set off the subtle marbling in the muted earth-tone colors of the tiles.*

A clean, open atmosphere is created by the classic pattern of the floor tile in this kitchen. The small diamond insets add a subtle element of design that works with the grid created by the large grout lines.

The delicate marbleized veining and high-gloss finish of ceramic tile add richness to the room and provide a practical and protective surface. Rectangular wall tiles feature a decaled border that runs throughout the room and defines the top of the dado; the smaller wall tiles visually draw the space together and keep the expansive room from seeming too large. The water-resistant ceramic tiles protect the walls from damaging water and steam.

Choosing the right tile

WALL TILES

Any wall that gets wet from being splashed or sprayed will benefit from a ceramic or natural tile surface. But don't limit ceramic tile applications strictly to these "wet surfaces." Ceramic tile can be used around doors and windows to add an artistic touch, or an interesting design element. Wall tiles are especially valuable when used to protect the bottom section of the wall, just below the chair rail. This area, sometimes called a dado, is usually located about the same height as the back of a dining chair. The dado area is often covered with ceramic tile to help protect the wall from rain-soaked clothes or muddy boots, as well as markings from chairs, tables, etc. Individual tiles can be used as accents within a larger design. Around tubs and showers, a tiled wall not only provides a decorative surface, but also one that is water-resistant, longer wearing and easier to clean.

Wall tiles are usually glazed and offer a wide variety of colors and designs. They are usually lighter and thinner than floor tiles, which makes an application on a vertical surface easier. The glaze ensures a water-resistant surface. For maximum water-resistance, use epoxy grout with wall tiles. Not only is this type of grout highly waterproof, it is also highly resistant to most stains.

A colorful geometric pattern, made of of bold, bright ceramic tiles, accentuates the unique shape of this shower. The ceramic tile provides a water-resistant surface for this stylish shower surround.

This elegant tiled entryway uses colors, textures and patterns to create a look that is simple and sophisticated. Off-white wall tiles set in a diagonal pattern and the use of larger wall tiles below the dado line help expand the sense of space in this small setting. The ceramic tile helps protect wall and floor surfaces from moisture and dirt that is dragged into this fashionable foyer.

WALL TILES

Ceramic tile is a long-wearing, waterproof surface that is also very attractive and easy to clean. Because wall tile is mounted on the wall, away from heavy traffic, the durability of the surface is not of as much importance. This means that for many wall applications, the selection of ceramic tiles that make effective wall tiles is even broader than when selecting floor tiles.

Wall tiles will often need to be finished around the edges with some kind of border or trim. Many manufacturers of wall tiles have specially shaped, matching border and trim pieces available. Border tiles are special tiles specifically shaped to finish off edges, form coves, and turn corners. There are a variety of different border tiles that can be used to finish a wall tile application. Cove tiles are curved at the bottom and are used along the bottom row of wall tile which adjoins the floor tile to create a smooth transition. There are trim pieces for sink corners, inside and outside wall corners and bullnose tile, which is used at the edge of a wall or top of a dado. Many wall tile manufacturers now offer decorative trim pieces to coordinate with their tile selections.

Creating wall and floor tile installations that match and are properly aligned can be very tricky. Many manufacturers offer predesigned packages that include floor and wall tiles and eliminate much of the guesswork involved in coordinating the two applications.

Photo courtesy of Sicis, Gabbianelli, Rex, Bardelli, Grazia, Mayo De Lucci, Italian Trade Commission - Tile Center in New York

(above) **Large wall tiles** *were used in this application to help balance and support the grand size and stature of the other architectural elements in the setting.*

(right) **Wall tiles, with the look of polished marble,** *provide an easy-to-clean, water-resistant surface.*

Photo courtesy of Monarch Tile Inc.

The coolness of polished marble finishes this room with long-lasting elegance from floor to ceiling. Finely detailed relief tiles enhance the sense of sophistication and gracefully divide the space so it is visually balanced.

A border of decorated wall tiles *frames the display shelves. The two-color design is repeated again on the back wall of the recessed shelves, which creates an interesting visual affect.*

Delicately detailed *trim and accent tiles add an elegant touch that is soft and subtle. Narrow, decorative accent tiles define the top of the dado on this wall, and visually divide the expanse of ceramic tiles.*

Seashells by the seashore *is the theme of this clever design scheme. Decorative border tiles coordinate with larger decorative wall tiles. The design pattern along the border tiles has been spot-glazed to add visual highlights and an interesting element of texture.*

WALL TILES

Ceramic wall tiles are an effective choice for use on deeply set windows where the ledges act as shelves for plants or other collectibles. Ceramic tiles also make an excellent choice for use around greenhouse windows. They absorb and reflect heat to the plants, and offer easy cleanup for water and dirt spills.

The classic charm of old-world Italy *is re-created in this bathroom using ceramic wall tiles with a marbleized finish. The vintage appeal of the ceramic tile and its protective and long-lasting physical qualities make this creation a true masterpiece.*

Large rectangular wall tiles *expand the sense of space in this contemporary kitchen. The geometric shapes and subtle colors in the borders give the area visual boundaries and continuity.*

The bold colors of this fire-resistant, ceramic facing contribute to the strong Southwestern influence in the styling of this room.

Choosing the right tile

WALL TILES

Because of their fire-resistant qualities, many types of ceramic tile are well suited to decorating different parts of a fireplace. The hearth can be given an attractive tile surface that is also a decorative part of a room's design. An ordinary mantel can be transformed into a focal point by finishing it with an artfully designed ceramic surface. A tiled mantel creates an interesting stage for various displays. The facing, or the area surrounding the opening in a fireplace, lends itself to many creative tile opportunities. Decorative tiles that complement and enhance the rest of the design can also be applied to the front of the chimney.

Softly textured relief tiles are used to establish the design motif of this fireplace facing. Because the decorative tiles are the same color as the background tiles, the design element is subtle and more sophisticated.

Fire-resistant ceramic tiles were used to form the attractive Art Deco design on the facing and the floor, in front of this fireplace. The sophisticated look of this setting is a perfect example of how a ceramic tile application can be both fun and functional.

Large ceramic floor and wall tiles are used to create a fire-resistant hearth and cover the front facing surface of this fireplace.

Ceramic tiles, designed to look like naturally aged stone, are combined with a rich wood frame to create this sleek and stylish fireplace. The fire-resistant qualities of the ceramic and marble facing also make this fireplace safe and more functional.

Decoratively painted tiles are used to create a vintage Victorian look for this fireplace. Plain tan tiles create the background for the decorative tiles on the facing, while black tiles make a fire-resistant surface on the floor in front of the fireplace.

COUNTER TILES

Ceramic tile makes an excellent material for finishing almost any surface in a bathroom or kitchen. In the kitchen, ceramic tile is highly effective around the sink and stove top. The hard, durable surface won't be affected by a sharp knife or a hot pan, and grease and food stains wipe off easily.

Although ceramic tile is a very durable material, it is still susceptible to chipping or cracking if heavy items are dropped on it, or a very hot or very cold object is placed directly on top of it for a long period of time.

The physical characteristics of counter tiles are very similar to those of wall tiles. Like wall tiles, counter tiles are available in an almost endless array of colors, shapes and sizes. They are glazed with a semigloss or high-gloss finish that maintains color intensity and makes them easy to clean.

Photo courtesy of WALKER ZANGER

Ceramic tiles are a wonderful way to put a waterproof surface around a wet area, such as the sink in a bathroom. This ceramic tile application also incorporates ceramic tiles as a design element in a border around the sink and in various configurations on the walls and floor.

*A **shiny, clean** ceramic tile surface gives this colorful countertop a special gleam. A collection of decorated tiles adds water-resistant protection to the wall behind the sink. The cheery design and sparkling appeal of the porcelain tile on the countertop and backsplash creates a setting that's bright and upbeat.*

(above) **A traditional checkerboard pattern** *is given an upscaled elegance with the addition of a border of thinner tiles that give this classic pattern a livelier new look. The busy pattern used on the countertop is balanced by a simpler, less active floor tile pattern.*

(inset) **Clean, white ceramic countertops** *are an excellent option in any kitchen. Here, the simple white counter space is a calm contrast to the lively tile application given to the front surface of these kitchen cabinets.*

COUNTER TILES

Ceramic counter tiles can be used to create a custom look. You can define the area behind the cooktop, the backsplash behind the sink or designate a workspace on a countertop.

Ceramic counter tiles are designed primarily for use on kitchen, bathroom and other similar types of countertops. They also make a decorative and durable surface for shelves, windowsills and tabletops. They are also an easy way to add a colorful accent to a design scheme.

As with wall tiles, there are specially shaped trim tiles for counters, which makes installation around edges, sinks, backsplashes and corners easier.

The versatility of ceramic tile allows you to create your own countertop design for a truly personalized look. The fine detail that can be accomplished with ceramic tiles is one benefit that makes this material really stand out. The more creative you can be with your installation, the more original and personalized your room will be.

(far left) **White on white** *makes a dramatic visual statement. The crisp white counter tiles are defined and made more visually dramatic by the wide, white grout lines.*

(left) **Decorative trim tiles** *give this counter tile installation an attractive edge. Lighter-colored tiles are used to define the work area on the top of the counter. Matching wall tiles are installed on an adjacent wall, at an angle, to distinguish between the two separate surfaces.*

(left) **A sea of small blue ceramic tiles** *inspires an aquatic theme in this spacious bathroom and spa. The water-resistant qualities of the tiles make them ideal for every application in the room.*

COUNTER TILES

Hand-painted trim tiles *border this countertop and reflect the painted design in the porcelain sink. The decorative design is also used on the walls and as a border around the mirror.*

Stylishly shaped trim tiles *and accent tiles with a delicate decorative design add a light, fresh look to this pastel powder room.*

Contrasting colored grout *defines the grid and makes it a decorative element in this countertop. The braided trim tile along the backsplash adds a distinctive design element to the water-resistant surface of the countertop.*

Coordinated tile sets *offer matching tiles for flat surfaces, edges and accents. This beautiful bathroom reflects the elegance ceramic tile is capable of bringing to a bathroom or any other setting.*

Beige and black with accents of brass *are the colors that comprise this sophisticated ceramic tile countertop. The metallic gold accent tile picks up the brass in the fixtures and frame of the mirror on the wall behind. Besides the wonderfully rich aesthetic quality, ceramic tile has the advantage of being water-resistant as well.*

Design
DESIGNING WITH TILE

The ideal ceramic or natural tile design delivers the perfect balance between functional needs and aesthetic pleasure. This is not difficult to achieve if you research the characteristics of the various types of tile and follow the basic rules of shape, size, color, texture, scale, pattern and rhythm. The vast selection of ceramic and natural tiles available offers a range of composition possibilities that is almost endless. By rearranging the basic building blocks of design you can compose a well-planned ceramic tile configuration that organizes the different parts of a space into one harmonious whole.

Begin planning your tile design by compiling examples of ceramic tile design schemes from books and magazines. Also collect paint, wallpaper and fabric samples that will need to coordinate with your ceramic tile design. Visit a tile showroom to see examples of tile types you are considering. Ask for samples to take home with you so you can view the tile in the proposed setting. Because of the durability and longevity of

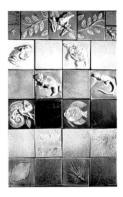

ceramic tile, you will probably be living with your selection for a long time, so choose colors and designs that will allow you to replace the furnishings or change the motif of the room.

Although grout is not considered as part of the design of the tile, it plays an important part is the overall look of a ceramic tile application. There are two design factors that you need to think about when selecting grout—the color and the width of the joint, or the space between tiles. Using a grout color that contrasts with the tiles will emphasize the grid pattern that forms as a result of the spacing between the tiles and the geometry of the design. This can create a stunning look, if done correctly. However, it will also make any flaws or irregularities in width or placement more prominent. To decrease the emphasis on the grid, choose a grout that matches the tile colors or one that will be almost neutral when compared to the tile. If you are installing decorative tiles, match the grout color to the background color, otherwise the grout will compete with the design for attention.

(opposite page) **Clever ceramic tile patterns** *allow you to create a tiled wall that looks like wallpaper. But the ceramic tile is water-resistant, washable and will last much longer.*

(left) **This all-white ensemble of ceramic floor** *tiles uses texture and patterns, as well as the contrast between glossy and matte tiles, to create the subtle visual styling of this tile application.*

Photo courtesy of Crossville Ceramics. Photo above courtesy of Ann Sacks Tile & Stone

33

SHAPE & SIZE

One of the primary principals of design is the way the shape and size of various elements in a design scheme relate to one another within the space. These elements should balance and complement each other. The size and shape of tiles used in various applications can also affect the feel, or ambience, of a room. For example, circular elements give a room a feeling of closure that can be comforting. Curved shapes help emphasize areas that you want to define, such as a shower area within a large bathroom. The most common tile shape available is square. Square tiles are the most versatile and the easiest to install. Other common shapes include rectangles, hexagons and octagons. Shape can also be accentuated with color. By using borders, stripes and contrasting colors, you can create dramatic shapes using square tiles.

The basic rule to follow when dealing with size in relation to ceramic tile application is—small tiles look good in small rooms and large tiles look better in large rooms. Large tiles tend to expand the size of the surface; small tiles tend to decrease it. If you are using more than one size tile in the same room, use large tiles on lower surfaces rather than on higher ones. Avoid tiling a countertop with tiles that are larger than the ones on the floor; this will make the room look awkward and top-heavy.

Photo courtesy of Monarch Tile Inc.

Decorative wall and trim tiles *add a colorful border around this inset alcove. The contrasting-colored tiles have a distinctive narrow rectangular shape that helps create a contrasting border that defines the shelf area.*

Photo courtesy of Marcia Corona, Italian Trade Commission - Tile Center in New York

Large ceramic floor tiles *expand the sense of space and add a water-resistant surface to this work area. The diagonal application enhances this sense of roominess. Smaller-sized tiles, on the walls and counter areas, contrast nicely with the larger floor tiles. Because there is more tiled area on the walls and counters, the smaller tiles are used here. Larger tiles, such as those used on the floor, would overwhelm the entire room.*

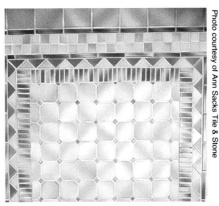

Custom tile designers *use a multitude of shapes, colors and sizes when creating an original tile design. This one-of-a-kind design will add originality and a hand-crafted appeal to any setting.*

Color, size and shape *all play an intricate part in this ceramic tile pattern.*

A delicate floral design *made from relief tile creates this ceramic tile border. The pattern is accentuated by the colorful glaze that has been applied.*

Colors have a dramatic effect *in this luxurious lavatory. The matching grout used on the marbled white tiles gives the tiled areas a larger unified look. When used with darker tiles, the light-colored grout lines define the tiles and make them look smaller.*

An original floor tile design *turns this marble floor into a modern-day masterpiece. The centerpiece of the design is a configuration that creates the illusion of an area rug in the center of the room. Pieces of tile resembling mosaic tiles are inset randomly throughout the floor pattern.*

COLOR

Color is the most influential element of basic design. The vast selection and intensity of colors available is one of the strongest advantages of ceramic tile. Color sets the mood in a setting— you feel color as well as see it. Color selection is very important to establishing the ambience of a room. Ceramic tiles are available in almost any color imaginable, and tile manufacturers regularly adjust their color selections to match current fashion trends. If you can't find the color you're looking for in a manufactured tile, custom colors can be created; ask your local tile distributor for details.

You can install colored tiles in a defined pattern, or place them randomly. The number of colors you put together in one design depends on the other elements in a room, such as the furniture, wallpaper and window treatments. The colors in your tile design must work with all of the design components in a setting. A monochromatic, or one-color, design scheme can have a soothing effect, but may become too monotonous. Analogous, or closely related, colors are always a safe combination. Complementary or contrasting colors intensify one another. A

multicolored design adds excitement, but can be too busy if overdone.

The placement of colors in relation to one another, and to the other elements in a room, affects the way they are perceived. Warm colors are comfortable and cozy, and make objects seem closer. Cool colors are refreshing and clean; they give the illusion of receding. The best interior design schemes combine both warm and cool colors and allow one color temperature to dominate. Light colors make a space seem larger, while darker colors minimize space. Dark floors can make a large room seem smaller and more intimate. A dark floor will help light furnishings stand out more, while a light floor will make the room seem larger and will help light furnishings blend into the overall design scheme.

Bold colors work best in small doses in smaller areas, such as entries or hallways. If an area has an alcove or niche that is an interesting focal point, it can be highlighted with a dramatic tile design.

Photo above courtesy of Selene Seltzer/Designs in Tile, Mt. Shasta, CA
This photo courtesy of Sicis, Italian Trade Commission - Tile Center in New York

*A **sense of motion and excitement** is created when complementary colors are used in conjunction with the right shapes. This tile application, featuring a beautiful six-pointed ceramic tile star, seems to radiate rings of blue hues from aqua to cobalt.*

(above) **The natural tone** of the wood cabinetry is complemented by the natural muted colors used in the ceramic tile accents on the wall behind the counter and across the front of the hood above the stove.

(left) **The soft colors** and rounded shape of the small ceramic tiles create the ambience of a textured area rug. Distinctive borders, made with narrow green tiles, help define the areas of the floor and reinforce the area rug illusion.

The hint of a checkerboard pattern adds an interesting accent to this lavish bathroom. The diagonal diamond pattern is repeated in the floor pattern of contrasting white grout and large rust and teal tiles.

Designing with tile

PATTERN & TEXTURE

Pattern and texture also contribute to the development of a decorating theme. Ceramic and natural tile adds a great deal of interest and character to any room; it can be matte, textured, patterned or sculptured, depending on the mood you're trying to create. Smooth textures and precise patterns create a more formal setting, while rough and random patterns are more suited to casual settings. Texture also affects the look of any color. Smooth surfaces will appear lighter and rough ones darker.

Ceramic tile can help reconfigure spaces. Tiles set in a diagonal pattern can change the perceived dimensions of a room, while curved or circular patterns add a feeling of openness and flow to a space. Repeating colors in a pattern and using the same colors in more than one area of a setting is another way to unify a look. You can create optical illusions by laying tile in different patterns or contrasting colors. Tile can be used to define individual areas in a room by using borders or changing colors.

Small, triangular-shaped tiles *create a lively diamondlike pattern of turquoise and black that pops against the sparkling white ceramic. Combining the small tiles with the contrasting white grout creates a textured, almost quilted effect.*

Blue and white Italian ceramic tiles *bring a taste of the old country to this kitchen. On the floor, small tiles create patterns that resemble one large floor tile. Each design is framed by solid white tiles, which reinforce the illusion of larger floor tiles and keep the space from feeling too crowded.*

The dominant white *of this bathroom is set off by the bold red checkerboard pattern and the thin green trim tiles. The vivid colors accentuate the ledge and make it seem larger than it really is.*

Planning this unusual pattern *took thought and imagination. The soothing shades of green and unusual tile shapes create an example of the unique pattern possibilities you can achieve working with ceramic tile.*

ARTISTIC EXPRESSIONS

Ceramic tile adds a unique personality to a space, and is one of the best ways to customize a home with a design element. Art tiles function to provide specialized graphic elements and options. Different types of art tiles include: decorated tiles, such as hand-painted and tiles with decals applied; mosaic tiles; relief tiles and tiles cut from natural stone. Art tiles are ideal for aesthetic applications, but are not as strong and durable as ceramic tiles made for walls and floors.

Hand-painted tiles are often created for tile shops by artists. Although most hand-painted tiles are made by professionals, you can paint your own and have them fired and glazed. They come in an array of decorative designs and can be used as individual accents in a variety of places, such as the backsplash behind a kitchen sink or interspersed within a solid color border that runs along a wall. Entire scenes can be painted on a group of tiles.

Mosaic tiles are some of the most colorful and versatile types of tile. These smaller, decoratively shaped tiles look striking in any setting. Mosaic tiles can be made of natural clay tile or hard porcelain tile, in either glazed or unglazed versions.

Tiles are not only made from fired clay, they are also made from other natural materials, like stone, slate and marble. Natural tiles create a comfortable, unique ambience in any setting.

Trend-setting ceramic tiles can help you achieve affordable elegance in any area. In this beautiful bathroom, dark green wall tiles with a marbleized high-gloss finish create a soothing ambience. Metallic gold decals were applied to matching green tiles, which were used to add attractive accents, as well as a border that is stylish and sophisticated.

Photo courtesy of Laufen Ceramic Tile. Photo above courtesy of Ann Sacks Tile & Stone

(top) **Clever use of texture and pattern** create a crisp, clean-looking kitchen. White ceramic counter tiles are combined with rope accent tiles and thick tile grout lines to create a flurry of visual activity in a seemingly calm setting.

(inset) **The arched alcove** above the stove and the rounded corners are accentuated by rope-style trim tiles in a complementary dark green color.

(left) **A decal of a soft pastel pattern** was applied to narrow border tiles, to help create a soothing setting for a relaxing soak in the tub. The rope styling of the ceramic trim tiles adds an element of texture, as well as a subtle visual accent.

41

DECORATED TILES

In addition to being glazed, tiles can also be decorated. Some decorated tiles are hand-painted, others have decals applied to them. Common themes for decorated tiles are animals and plants. Many times local artists can be hired to paint tiles to match wallpaper, fabric or an original design or pattern.

Decorated tiles can also be used in many outdoor areas. They are ideal for spa and pool applications—a mural of a scenic landscape or a delightful abstract design of shapes and colors can have a dynamic impact on a poolside setting.

Photo courtesy of Florida Tile Industries, Inc.

High-gloss, hand-painted color *reinforces the relief image cast in the design of the tile. Decorative border tiles pick up the same colors used in the decorated tile and carry them throughout the setting.*

The artistic value *of tiles is celebrated in this display of age-worn, hand-painted ceramic tiles.*

Photo courtesy of Vietri

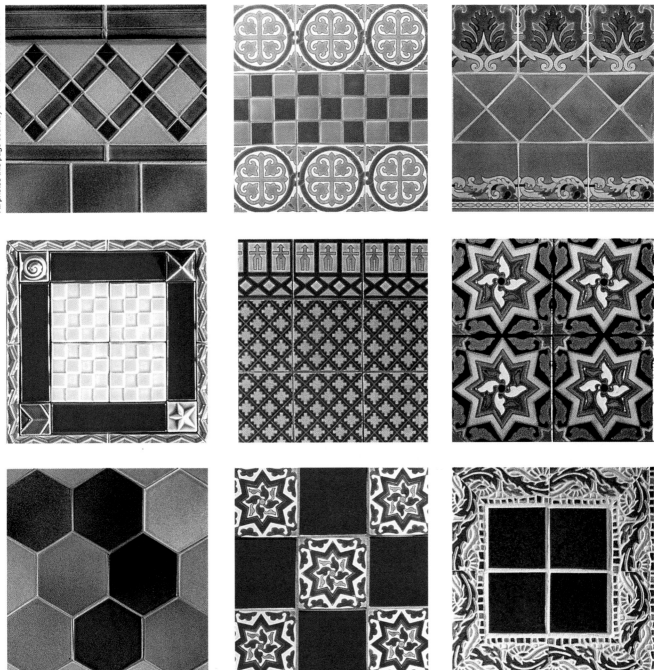

This amazing assortment *of ceramic art tiles illustrates just a few of the many innovative options available today. A considerable impact can be achieved with a few decorated tiles. You can also combine large groups of matching, patterned tiles to create a wallpapered effect, which can also have a dramatic and stunning impact. Decorative tiles are appropriate in any entrance area, at the front or back of a house. They are also used to define the top or bottom edge of a dado. Decorative tiles also are an interesting backdrop for a display of china or glass.*

DECORATED TILES

Hand-painted tiles are usually created for tile shops by local artists. You can also find hand-painted tiles at craft fairs and art shows. These one-of-a-kind creations are a great way to customize and add charm and personality to a kitchen or bar.

Hand-painted tiles can be set as individual accents in a backsplash wall or counter, or entire scenes can be painted on a group of tiles. Painted tiles are usually too fragile to be used in a floor installation but they are ideal as accents or installed in groups to form a pattern or scenic illustration.

Decal tiles are a less expensive alternative to hand-painted tile, yet they still have that special hand-finished quality and are just as attractive. Decals can be applied to almost any tiles; colored, patterned or plain. Hand-painting achieves the best results when used on plain tiles.

Common themes for decal tiles are flowers, animals, vegetables and graphic symbols. These images are permanently applied to the tiles through a firing process done at the tile store. Decal tiles are fragile, like painted tile, and should be used on wall applications and lightly used areas of countertops.

These hand-colored, multitile panels *create a scenic mural on this kitchen wall that resembles the painted tiles that adorned the walls of late 19th-century Europe. From this kitchen alcove, the realistic impact of this mural creates the illusion of looking out an actual window.*

Decorated tiles can be used to great practical and decorative effect in many areas around the house. Kitchen and bathroom sinks need a backsplash to protect the wall behind them. A small panel of decorative tiles is one way to add interest to a backsplash. More delicate, decorated tiles can sometimes be used on the floor in small quantities, in areas that don't get heavy use. For example, on the floor in front of the sink, several decorated tiles are grouped together to create a mat effect. The patterned area should be wider and deeper than the actual sink.

45

NATURAL TILES

One type of tile that has gained recent popularity in interior design is natural tile. This type of tile is cut from natural stone, such as slate, marble and limestone. Modern sawing techniques have made natural stone widely available for domestic use. The thinner sliced stone is cheaper and lighter to transport and install.

Terra-cotta tiles are also called earthenware tiles. These handmade tiles have a more rustic look than quarry tiles, which are flatter and more regular in shape. The most significant difference between terra-cotta and quarry tile is the temperature they are fired at; quarry tiles are fired at a much higher temperature, so they are less porous than terra-cotta.

Natural tiles also add a textural contrast that increases their dramatic effect. Large natural tiles can add a sense of permanence and stability to a room. For example, large marble tiles used on both the entryway floor and the floors of the adjacent rooms can visually expand the space. Slate is another natural stone that can be used to create a hard-wearing and dramatic floor. It has a soft, rippling texture that adds an attractive touch and also helps prevent slipping.

Massive buff and blue marble floor tiles are laid on the diagonal. Wall tiles of the same marble extend the grace and grandeur of this Euro-style bathroom up the walls and into the hall.

A terra-cotta tile floor is enlivened by small, patterned inset tiles. Terra-cotta is available in many color variations and shapes. The area the terra-cotta tiles originate from will determine the coloring of the tiles. Some shades are richer and darker, while others are softer and browner.

(inset) **Terra-cotta tiles** create a rustic, natural-looking floor. In this application, smaller terra-cotta tiles were given a decorative decal and used as a design accent.

The rose-colored and buff-colored marble tiles *impart a formal ambience in this sitting area. Inlaid pieces of the buff-colored marble are used to create an intricate border.*

47

NATURAL TILES

Many types of natural stone are suitable for both indoor and outdoor use. Natural stone makes a good surface for outdoor terraces and patios, as well as porches, conservatories, kitchens and hallways. When used in both interior and exterior settings, natural stone tiles can help make the transition between the interior space and the outdoors smooth and graceful.

When installing natural tile outdoors, take into account the climactic conditions of the setting, especially if the climate includes days with freezing temperatures. You can seal natural stone and slate tiles to help preserve their original appearance.

To add textural interest to a monochromatic natural tile application, sculpted tile borders, of natural-looking ceramic, were added to enhance the basic design. The natural stone, as well as the ceramic tiles, impart water-resistant protection to the wall and exude a warm ambience.

A sunny, poolside patio is surfaced with water-resistant terra-cotta tiles. The rough, uneven surface of the natural tile creates a textured, slip-resistant surface that is a safer option for this outdoor wet area.

The provincial look of this terra-cotta floor is embellished with a decorative accent tile in every corner.

The uneven textures and muted, earthy colors of natural stone are captured in the rustic look of these tiles. Natural-finish tiles can be used for various purposes and effects. Marble tiles appear luxurious, and they're also very hard-wearing. Unglazed terra-cotta imparts interesting tones and textures to a surface. Natural tiles are individually shaped and look as though they were cut by hand. Their subtle color variations add to the authenticity of the look and charm.

MOSAIC TILES

A mosaic design is the combination of small pieces of multicolored materials such as clay, marble, ceramic or glass, which are fired for a long time at a high temperature. Mosaic tiles are very dense and hard, and can withstand freezing. The small pieces are known as tesserae and the labor of assembling them into a pattern or picture is the difficult and costly aspect of mosaic work. The most common shapes of mosaic tiles are squares, octagons and hexagons—special original designs are also available. Generally, mosaic tiles are sold back-mounted on mesh sheets.

The number of mosaic floors that have survived intact, in entryways, halls, porches and pathways, is a testimony to the toughness and longevity of the material. Mosaic tiles are used to create intricate and elaborate designs. At its most detailed, a mosaic can be almost like a painting. The well-defined, sophisticated look of a mosaic design can often stand by itself as a unique work of art.

Mosaics are good for walls, floors, countertops and many other tile applications. They can be used both indoors and out, and in wet and dry locations. Mosaic tiles are especially effective in entryways, alcoves and other small areas where the

brilliant colors and the intricacy of a mosaic design become a visual focal point. Around fireplaces, they can add a striking design to a fireplace setting. Mosaic tile applied around a fireplace will also protect the tiled areas from stray sparks.

Mosaic tiles can be arranged in swirling and circular lines, presenting endless design and color possibilities. You can achieve dramatic results when mosaic tile is applied as a border design, in long, unbroken stretches, where the motion and rhythm of the design can gain momentum.

(right) **This intricately laid** *mosaic tile floor has the appearance of a rich Persian floor rug. The design uses small tiles to create a delicate floral design over this entire floor area.*

(above) **These exuberant patterns** *are modern examples of mosaic tile designs. Each tile contains several pieces of colored stone, and the process of making mosaic tiles is as labor-intensive today as it was centuries ago.*

(left) **Very small ceramic tiles** *have a visual impact similar to true mosaic tiles, when applied as a surface to the floor and sides of the tub in this small bathroom setting.*

51

RELIEF TILES

Relief tiles are made by forming a pattern into the tiles, so that the design either stands out from the surface, which is called a *relief*, or is inset, called a *counter-relief*. Relief tiles can be placed randomly within plain tiling, be arranged in groups or function as panels.

When using relief tiles in a tile installation, use common sense when choosing relief patterns that might be dangerous in certain locations. For example, sharp protrusions should be avoided in locations like corners and low areas of the wall where a child might be injured.

Contemporary tile manufacturers *have started producing specialized tiles with the techniques of the old artisans while utilizing current technology. These handmade ceramic tiles with a relief design are suitable for kitchen, bathroom, entryway and fireplace applications. The tile assortments available to choose from include fruits, vegetables, birds, flowers, sea life, geometric designs and mural bouquets.*

Some relief tiles are a machine-pressed design, others are produced in plaster molds. The molds allow for duplication and uniformity of the individual designs which can be carried throughout an entire interior design theme. After the mold is made, a polyurethane master tile is used to make plaster castings as needed. The castings are then kiln-fired at very high temperatures, glaze applied and tiles fired again to melt the glaze and bond it with the surface of the clay.

A PORTFOLIO OF

CERAMIC
&NATURAL
TILE
IDEAS

A decorative tile border separates the beige and white checkerboard from the glossy white tiles above. The wall tiles above the border have been set diagonally for added visual interest. The solid beige floor complements the checkerboard scheme, while setting a quiet and soothing tone for the room.

TILE IN THE BATHROOM

Ceramic tile provides both beauty and utility in one of the most heavily used areas of the home. It's a practical choice for bath and shower areas, which are constantly exposed to water and moisture. Tile won't rot or warp, even under continual dousing, and spilled water is easily mopped or wiped away.

Polished glazed tile presents a beautiful, sparkling, water-resistant surface for your bathroom walls and counters. Slip-resistant tile for the floors ensures safety for your family and guests. The physical characteristics of ceramic tile also deter germ and bacteria growth. Be sure to use mildew-resistant grout for all tile installation in the bathroom. This particular type of grout will result in a longer-lasting installation, as well as a healthier and more attractive bathroom.

Opportunities abound for decorative bathroom tile applications, from unique moldings around showers and baths, to intricate, carefully inlaid mosaic floor patterns. Since small tiles provide a more slip-resistant footing than large tiles, a bathroom floor is the perfect place to plan and install a mosaic floor surface. This ancient style of flooring can range from a simple decorative pattern to a complex work of art.

There are tiles for your bathroom that match every style and budget. A professional tile installer can advise you on the best way to proceed, and also on how to use the layout of your bathroom to maximum effect. However you proceed, your investment will pay off in compliments from guests, personal satisfaction and the increased value of your home.

The decorative ribbons *near the ceiling and above the washbasin frame the smooth white wall tiles and provide a transition to the narrow, vertically striped tiles below. The large checkerboard floor pattern provides a visual balance to this inviting powder blue bath.*

A medley of different tiles coordinates to create this classically arranged bath. The cheerful design provides a welcome greeting in the morning.

(right) **Deep, dark tile** *provides the perfect setting for the sleek lines of this pedestal sink. The decorative gold braiding beautifully accents the brass fixtures.*

Photo above courtesy of Laufen Ceramic Tile. Photo left and opposite page courtesy of Crossville Ceramics.

Distinctive floor tiles *form a checkerboard pattern in various sizes, linking the bathroom with the glass-enclosed shower. Large wall tiles are used to help keep splashes under control.*

(left) **A classic checkerboard pattern** provides a striking backdrop for this compact bath. The small tiles create a busy design that visually pulls the walls and floors closer together.

(right) **A floral pattern** *repeated along the wall is coupled with a vintage armoire. Both elements contribute an airy, spring feeling to this bath.*

Photo courtesy of American Olean

Take a relaxing bath or shower in *this sumptuously furnished room. From the tiled artwork on the wall to the relief molding, mosaic borders and tiled floor, this room is a treat for the eyes.*

Photo courtesy of WALKER ZANGER

An intricate mosaic floor is *the striking centerpiece of this room. It is complemented by columns in a matching design that border the mirror. Beautiful marble and rich copper fixtures round out this memorable ensemble.*

The light, decorative tile pattern surrounding this kitchen wall and overhead rack is achieved by mosaics, border tile and larger decorative tiles. The pattern helps unite this large kitchen, and also provides a visual contrast to the dark marbled stovetop in the center of the room. Tiled counters and floors are ready to catch any spills.

TILE IN THE KITCHEN

Ceramic tile has been a favorite in the kitchen for generations, and for good reason. Tile offers a durable countertop surface that resists many of the scratches and knocks from heavy pans that often damage other, conventional surfaces. Tile is also heat-resistant, so you can set a warm pan down without worrying about melting or scorching. And with all the sauces, main courses and desserts traveling from stovetop to counter and back, placing tile directly around cooking areas ensures a sanitary, easy-to-clean workspace. Tile also works wonderfully underneath cupboards, behind ovens and burners, or wherever spatters and spills are likely to occur.

Tile in the kitchen can also add a decorative touch to one of the busiest rooms in the home, without cluttering valuable space or compromising efficiency. Kitchen walls and the spaces around sinks, vents and windows offer plenty of "canvas" on which to project your design ideas. Try specialty tiles like relief moldings, hand-painted tiles and border trim to add a dash of excitement. You can use a tile application on the walls to complement an existing floor or countertop pattern. No matter where your ideas take you, it's a solid bet that there is an appropriate type of tile. Even a simple tile application can add a personal touch to a kitchen space, and with a little planning, a coordinated tile design can transform a humdrum kitchen into a visual focal point for creative cooking.

(above) **Multicolored tiles** *used underneath cupboards and near the stove ensure easy cleanup of kitchen spills. The light brown floor tiles stand up against mobile furniture and constant foot traffic.*

(left) **Natural earth-tone tiles** *provide the foundation for this impressive kitchen and connecting entryway. The rough, natural texture of the tile complements the grand stone arch and Old World decor.*

Photo courtesy of LATCO Products

(right) **A practical, muted tile pattern** *in this spacious kitchen creates a unique textured effect along the backsplash, countertops and island worksurface.*

(below) **Here, the classic pattern** *employed on the wall is echoed in the floor design. The two tile applications work together, creating harmony and balance in this dignified, efficient kitchen.*

This photo courtesy of Crystal Cabinet Works Inc. Photo opposite page courtesy of Rubble Tile, Florida Tile Industries, Inc.

Decorative tiles *offer the right accent for this colorful country theme. The checkerboard pattern makes this large kitchen floor seem smaller and more comfortable.*

(right) **Decorative braided** trim tiles accent the countertop edges. The braided tile over the stovetop complements and enhances the unique arched fixtures of this kitchen.

(below) **A utilitarian,** easy-to-clean floor and countertop are teamed with a tasteful wall pattern to create a kitchen setting that is pleasing to look at and very functional.

Photo courtesy of LATCO Products

Photo courtesy of American Olean

Cool white tile *gives this kitchen a bright, clean sparkle. The wire chairs, straw seats and glass table add an exciting and bold contrast, while the dark green wallpaper balances the tone of the room.*

The natural earth-tone color of this tile acts as the perfect foundation for this elegant dining room.

TILE IN COMMON LIVING AREAS

Common living areas of your home such as living rooms, dining rooms and entryways can gain appreciably from the durability and style of ceramic and natural tile. Entryways welcome visitors to your home and to your sense of style. Well-chosen tile patterns can visually connect these areas to other rooms in the home. And in heavy-traffic areas, tile wears better and stays good-looking longer than most other surface options, like wood, vinyl or carpet.

Dining rooms should be able to handle any situation, from formal dining and entertaining to the daily family meal. Placing tile here can help you achieve the versatility needed for all of these activities. Large, lightly textured natural tiles evoke an atmosphere of European spaciousness and elegance, yet are practical enough for everyday use. Natural-looking terra-cotta tiles can help tone down large dining areas and make them feel more comfortable and rustic. Combine these arrangements with elements like accent spotlighting, and you can provide an opulent and unique dining atmosphere for your family and friends.

Tile also adds variety to a living room, family room or den arrangement. Different styles or patterns can distinguish separate areas of the living room (children's area, TV area, fireplace, etc.). Or, use one style throughout and place Persian or Oriental rugs in various spots to achieve the atmosphere and feeling you desire.

You can use the contrast between gloss and matte surfaces to create an interesting pattern that doesn't upset the neutral harmony of this coordinated dining room set.

Photos on both pages courtesy of Crossville Ceramics

(above) **The natural muted color** *of the tile serves to link this cozy breakfast and coffee space to the sunny outdoor deck just beyond the French doors.*

(below) **This tile design** *is a fitting accompaniment to the eclectic mood of this dining and entertainment nook.*

Photo courtesy of Laufen Ceramic Tile

After a brisk swim, the tiled floor in this rustic space helps provide a great place to warm up and enjoy refreshments.

A compact urban space gets a stylish, European makeover with a mosaic wall tile application behind the wine glasses. A frame of solid color surrounds the floor pattern that designates the dining area.

Photo courtesy of Trade Commission of Spain

A delicate central floor motif creates an assertive visual focal point to this simple dining room. The natural look and texture of the floor combines with the wire furniture and nearby plants to create the feeling of an outdoor patio.

Wide grout lines *emphasize the shape of the tiles and add to the look of this classic floor plan. The open pattern complements the spacious feeling of the arched hallway and light wall color.*

(left) **An inviting diamond arrangement** *of floor tile greets visitors. The hard-working tile keeps outdoor dirt from spreading, and bridges the transition to the adjacent living room.*

(below) **Pastel floor tiles** *blend in seamlessly with the painted walls and weathered furniture. Tile colors and shades can be found to match almost any decorating scheme.*

(left) **Large terra-cotta tile** uses dark grout to complement the spacious, exotic feel of this European villa-style living room. A large rug and numerous plants soften the overall ambience.

(below) **The rich Old World atmosphere** of this plush, romantic sitting room is balanced by the cool tile arrangement underfoot. Small aqua mosaics are teamed with large tiles in an interesting offset pattern.

Photo courtesy of Emil Bisazza, Vogel-Muela, Italian Trade Commission - Tile Center in New York

(above) **Large earth-colored tiles** *create the background, while various activity areas are defined by mosaic borders and diamond shapes in this spacious dining room.*

Large ceramic floor tiles of *pebble beige and malachite green create an elegant entry area. The large size of the tiles and the open, diagonal pattern of the tiles help open the space visually, while the durable ceramic provides a protective surface in this formal foyer.*

(below) **Beige tones** in the walls and furniture of this monochromatic living room are gently supported by the matching floor color.

Photo courtesy of Monarch Tile Inc.

(above) **A large tiled surround** complements the weathered look of this fireplace. The tile also protects the mantel from heat, soot and the occasional stray spark.

(left) **This bold, ordered tile pattern** brings a distinguished atmosphere to this formal receiving area. The elegant furnishings are visually supported by the strength and stability of the floor tile.

The dark grays *of this patterned floor design are echoed in the tile under and around the fireplace mantel. They offer a visual contrast to the reddish hues of the surrounding walls and accessories.*

Photo courtesy of Florida Tile Industries, Inc.

Photo courtesy of Crossville Ceramics

(left) **Sleek, polished tiles** *welcome visitors to the brightly lit foyer of this contemporary room.*

Photo courtesy of Florida Tile Industries, Inc.

Simple black-and-white *geometric designs often have the boldest impact, as this living room floor demonstrates.*

87

Inset photo opposite page courtesy of Susan Beere with John Conrad, Encinitas, CA, Tile Heritage Foundation

Photo courtesy of Featherock - United States Pumice

Cool blue tiles cover the entry steps and line the inside of this customized pool, while terra-cotta tiles cover the outer walkways. The differing textures and colors visually distinguish these separate outdoor environments. Natural pumice rocks and flowers provide additional visual interest.

TILE OUTDOORS

The benefits of ceramic and natural tile aren't confined to the inside of your home. Outdoor areas such as patios, swimming pools and water gardens are perfect places for tile. Tile produces a more welcoming and comfortable surface than brick or concrete. Terra-cotta tile on the floor of a screened-in porch, sun room or entryway can ease the shift from an indoor room to an outdoor setting. The continuity of the tile will make the outdoor area seem more integrated with the home as a whole. Since climates and needs vary, consult with a tile professional to determine which type of weather-resistant outdoor tile is recommended for your particular situation.

Around the swimming pool, tile is a traditional choice that offers both a beautiful decorative look to the surrounding poolside and a practical way to add a slip-resistant surface and keep poolside accidents under control. Borders around hot tubs, whirlpools and saunas are an easy way to tie different recreational areas together with a common design theme.

A tiled footpath or alcove is an enchanting addition to your garden that can lend your backyard a quiet, Victorian elegance. Combine these elements with borders around water gardens or flower beds and you can create a unique, relaxing retreat from the modern world.

The rich tile pattern re-creates the look of an area rug and defines the center of this beautifully sunlit outdoor alcove. The formal appeal of the tile makes it an appropriate setting for breakfast, afternoon tea or a romantic dinner alfresco.

(left) **The enduring beauty** *of ceramic tile is clearly evident in the crisp colors and bold designs of this inviting whirlpool.*

(below) **This tour de force** *of tile centers around an inventive mosaic design on the bottom of the swimming pool. Black and gold glazed tile borders the steps to the smaller pool above. Natural tile is used for the terrace floors, steps and surrounding walkways.*

*A **unique floral print tile*** and dark border define this terra-cotta
walkway. The surrounding plant life creates a colorful contrast to the tile.

Alternating black and white *tiles, diagonally positioned, create a
striking effect that emphasizes the linear continuity between the pool and
the terraced steps, which lead up to an old-fashioned tiled shower area.
The same striking border is used along the inside wall of the pool.*

The dazzling tiles *of this Art Deco-styled waterfall transform water and sun into a brilliant display of color.*

(right) **Natural colored tiles** wind their way around this ornate, delightful water garden and blend in peacefully with the lush surroundings.

Darker tile helps to offset this wading area from the rest of this large swimming pool, while a decorative inner border design stylistically bonds these two areas together. The natural tile bordering the entire area offers a slip-resistant footing for swimmers and guests.

*The large **terra-cotta tiles** of this sun-drenched terrace provide a rustic, versatile foundation for a variety of uses. The sunken area easily accommodates a large table and chairs, and offers a grand view of the tile-floored swimming pool and textured pool deck below.*

LIST OF CONTRIBUTORS

We'd like to thank the following companies for providing the photographs used in this book:

American Olean
1000 Cannon Avenue
Lansdale, PA 19446
(215) 393-2237

Ann Sacks Tile & Stone
8120 N.E. 33rd Drive
Portland, OR 97211
East Coast: (212) 463-0492
West Coast: (503) 331-7320

Crossville Ceramics
P.O. Box 1168
Crossville, TN 38557
(800) 221-9093

Crystal Cabinet Works, Inc.
1100 Crystal Drive
Princeton, MN 55371
(612) 389-4187

EMILCERAMICA
222 S.W. 15 Road
Miami, FL 33129
(305) 858-8242

Featherock, Inc.
United States Pumice Co.
20219 Bahama Street
Chatsworth, CA 91311
(800) 423-3037

Florida Tile Industries, Inc.
P.O. Box 447
Lakeland, FL 33566
(941) 284-4048

Heat-N-Glo Fireplace Products, Inc.
6665 W. Hwy. 13
Savage, MN 55378
(612) 890-8367

Italian Trade Commission
Tile Center
499 Park Avenue
New York, NY 10022
(212) 980-1500

LATCO Products
2943 Gleneden Street
Los Angeles, CA 90039
(213) 664-1171

Laufen Ceramic Tile
P.O. Box 6600
Tulsa, OK 74156-0600
(800) 758-TILE

Lilypons Water Gardens
7000 Lilypons Road
Buckeystown, MD 21717
(301) 874-5503

M.E. Tile Co.
400 E. Sibley Blvd.
Harvey, IL 60426
(708) 210-3229

Monarch Tile Inc.
834 Rickwood Rd.
Florence, AL 35630
(205) 764-6181

Rubble Tile
6001 Culligan Way
Minnetonka, MN 55345
(612) 938-2599

Selene Seltzer/Designs in Tile
Box 358
Mt. Shasta, CA 96067
(916) 926-2629

Tile Heritage Foundation
P.O. Box 1850
Healdsburg, CA 95448

Trade Commission of Spain
2655 LeJeune Road
Coral Gables, FL 33134
(305) 446-4387

Travis Industries
10850 117th Place N.E.
Kirkland, WA 98033
(206) 827-9505

United States Ceramic Tile Co.
P.O. Box 338
10233 Sandyville Rd. S.E.
East Sparta, OH 44626
(216) 866-5531

VIETRI, INC.
P.O. Box 460
Hillsborough, NC 27278
(919) 732-5933

WALKER ZANGER
8901 Bradley Avenue
Sun Valley, CA 91352
(818) 504-0235